floral SUNCATCHER

EASY

Finished Size: 8" (20.5 cm) diameter

SHOPPING LIST

Thread (Lace Weight)

LACE 0

- ☐ 70 yards (64 meters)

Crochet Hook

- ☐ Steel, size 7 (1.65 mm)
  or size needed for gauge

Additional Supplies

- ☐ 8" (20.5 cm) Metal ring
- ☐ 1/8" (3 mm) Ribbon (optional)

GAUGE INFORMATION

Gauge Swatch: 1¾" (4.5 cm)
(from point to point)

Work same as Suncatcher, page 4, through Rnd 3: 36 dc.

STITCH GUIDE

DOUBLE CROCHET 2 TOGETHER ***(abbreviated dc2tog)*** (uses next 2 sts)

★ YO, insert hook in **next** st, YO and pull up a loop, YO and draw through 2 loops on hook; repeat from ★ once **more**, YO and draw through all 3 loops on hook **(counts as one dc)**.

DOUBLE CROCHET 3 TOGETHER ***(abbreviated dc3tog)*** (uses next 3 sts)

★ YO, insert hook in **next** st, YO and pull up a loop, YO and draw through 2 loops on hook; repeat from ★ 2 times **more**, YO and draw through all 4 loops on hook **(counts as one dc)**.

CLUSTER (uses next 4 dc)

★ YO, insert hook in **next** dc, YO and pull up a loop, YO and draw through 2 loops on hook; repeat from ★ 3 times **more**, YO and draw through all 5 loops on hook.

SUNCATCHER

Ch 10; join with slip st to form a ring.

Rnd 1 (Right side)**:** Ch 3 **(counts as first dc, now and throughout)**, 23 dc in ring; join with slip st to first dc: 24 dc.

Rnd 2: Ch 3, 4 dc in same st as joining, ch 2, skip next 3 dc, ★ 5 dc in next dc, ch 2, skip next 3 dc; repeat from ★ around; join with slip st to first dc: 30 dc.

Rnd 3: Ch 3, dc in next dc, (dc, ch 3, dc) in next dc, dc in next 2 dc, ch 2, ★ dc in next 2 dc, (dc, ch 3, dc) in next dc, dc in next 2 dc, ch 2; repeat from ★ around; join with slip st to first dc: 36 dc.

Rnd 4: Ch 3, dc in next 2 dc, ch 2, 3 dc in center ch of next ch-3, ch 2, dc in next 3 dc, ch 2, ★ dc in next 3 dc, ch 2, 3 dc in center ch of next ch-3, ch 2, dc in next 3 dc, ch 2; repeat from ★ around; join with slip st to first dc: 54 dc.

quick THREAD PROJECTS

Brighten your life with a little bit of thread crochet. Add a lacy edging to a hand towel, make a pretty cover for a tissue box, or top a window with a wispy valance. You'll love how quick and easy these projects are!

LEISURE ARTS, INC.
Maumelle, Arkansas

Rnd 5: Ch 3, dc in next 2 dc, ch 2, 2 dc in next dc, dc in next dc, 2 dc in next dc, ch 2, dc in next 3 dc, ch 3, ★ dc in next 3 dc, ch 2, 2 dc in next dc, dc in next dc, 2 dc in next dc, ch 2, dc in next 3 dc, ch 3; repeat from ★ around; join with slip st to first dc: 66 dc.

Rnd 6: Ch 3, dc in next 2 dc, ch 2, 2 dc in next dc, dc in next 3 dc, 2 dc in next dc, ch 2, dc in next 3 dc, ch 4, ★ dc in next 3 dc, ch 2, 2 dc in next dc, dc in next 3 dc, 2 dc in next dc, ch 2, dc in next 3 dc, ch 4; repeat from ★ around; join with slip st to first dc: 78 dc.

Rnd 7: Ch 3, dc in next 2 dc, ch 2, dc2tog, dc in next 3 dc, dc2tog, ch 2, dc in next 3 dc, ch 5, ★ dc in next 3 dc, ch 2, dc2tog, dc in next 3 dc, dc2tog, ch 2, dc in next 3 dc, ch 5; repeat from ★ around; join with slip st to first dc: 66 dc.

Rnd 8: Ch 3, dc in next 2 dc, ch 2, dc2tog, dc in next dc, dc2tog, ch 2, dc in next 3 dc, ch 7, ★ dc in next 3 dc, ch 2, dc2tog, dc in next dc, dc2tog, ch 2, dc in next 3 dc, ch 7; repeat from ★ around; join with slip st to first dc: 54 dc and 6 ch-7 sps.

Rnd 9: Ch 3, dc in next 2 dc, ch 2, dc3tog, ch 2, dc in next 3 dc, ch 5, 2 dc in next ch-7 sp, ch 5, ★ dc in next 3 dc, ch 2, dc3tog, ch 2, dc in next 3 dc, ch 5, 2 dc in next ch-7 sp, ch 5; repeat from ★ around; join with slip st to first dc.

Rnd 10: Ch 3, dc in next 2 dc, ch 2, dc in next dc, ch 2, dc in next 3 dc, ch 5, dc in next dc, ch 2, dc in next dc, ch 5, ★ dc in next 3 dc, ch 2, dc in next dc, ch 2, dc in next 3 dc, ch 5, dc in next dc, ch 2, dc in next dc, ch 5; repeat from ★ around; join with slip st to first dc.

Rnd 11: Ch 3, dc in next 2 dc, skip next dc, dc in next 3 dc, ch 7, 6 dc in next ch-2 sp, ch 7, skip next ch-5 sp, ★ dc in next 3 dc, skip next dc, dc in next 3 dc, ch 7, skip next ch-5 sp, 6 dc in next ch-2 sp, ch 7, skip next ch-5 sp; repeat from ★ around; join with slip st to first dc: 72 dc and 12 ch-7 sps.

Rnd 12: Ch 2, dc in next dc, dc2tog twice, ch 9, skip next ch-7 sp, dc in next 2 dc, (ch 2, dc in next 2 dc) twice, ch 9, skip next ch-7 sp, ★ dc2tog 3 times, ch 9, skip next ch-7 sp, dc in next 2 dc, (ch 2, dc in next 2 dc) twice, ch 9, skip next ch-7 sp; repeat from ★ around; join with slip st to first dc: 54 dc and 12 ch-9 sps.

Rnd 13: Ch 2, dc2tog, ch 4, sc in next ch-9 sp, ch 4, 2 dc in each of next 2 dc, (ch 5, 2 dc in each of next 2 dc) twice, ch 4, sc in next ch-9 sp, ch 4, ★ dc3tog, ch 4, sc in next ch-9 sp, ch 4, 2 dc in each of next 2 dc, (ch 5, 2 dc in each of next 2 dc) twice, ch 4, sc in next ch-9 sp, ch 4; repeat from ★ around; join with slip st to first dc: 90 sts and 12 ch-5 sps.

Rnd 14: Ch 12, work Cluster, (ch 4, sc in next ch-5 sp, ch 4, work Cluster) twice, ch 9, skip next sc, ★ dc in next dc, ch 9, work Cluster, (ch 4, sc in next ch-5 sp, ch 4, work Cluster) twice, ch 9, skip next sc; repeat from ★ around; join with slip st to third ch of beginning ch-12, finish off.

Finishing

Cut a length of ribbon 30" (76 cm) long **plus** the length you want for the hanger, **or** crochet a chain of the same length.
Using photo as a guide for placement, page 2, weave ribbon or chain through ch-sps **and** around 8" (20.5 cm) metal ring, leaving tails of equal length and adjusting loops evenly. Tie a knot close to ring; then tie ends in a knot to make hanger.

Design by Shobha Govindan.

vintage "DRAWERS"

Finished Size: 5" wide x 7" high (12.5 cm x 18 cm) EASY

SHOPPING LIST

Thread (Lace Weight)

Grandpa's Trunks:

- ☐ Blue - 110 yards (101 meters)

Gentleman's Trunks:

- ☐ White - 70 yards (64 meters)
- ☐ Blue - 40 yards (36.5 meters)

Lady's Bloomers:

- ☐ White - 135 yards (123.5 meters)
- ☐ Blue - 10 yards (9 meters)

Crochet Hook

- ☐ Steel, size 6 (1.8 mm) **or** size needed for gauge

Additional Supplies

Grandpa's and Gentleman's Trunks:

- ☐ ¼" (6 mm) Buttons - 2
- ☐ Sewing needle and thread

GAUGE INFORMATION

18 dc and 8 rnds/rows = 2" (5 cm)

Gauge Swatch: 2" (5 cm) square

Ch 20.

Row 1: Dc in fourth ch from hook and in each ch across **(3 skipped chs count as first dc)**: 18 dc.

Rows 2-8: Ch 3 **(counts as first dc)**, turn; dc in next dc and in each dc across.

Finish off.

GRANDPA'S TRUNKS

Body

With Blue, ch 80; being careful **not** to twist ch, join with slip st to form a ring.

Rnd 1 (Right side)**:** Ch 1, sc in same ch as joining and in each ch around; join with slip st to first sc: 80 sc.

Note: Loop a short piece of thread around any stitch to mark Rnd 1 as **right** side.

Hanging Loop: Ch 16; slip st in first ch to form a loop, **turn**; 24 sc in loop, slip st in first sc of Rnd 1.

Work in Back Loops Only throughout *(Fig. 2, page 47)*.

Rnd 2: Ch 3 (**counts as first dc, now and throughout**), dc in next 19 sc, ch 1, dc in next 40 sc, ch 1, dc in last 20 sc; join with slip st to first dc: 80 dc and 2 chs.

Rnd 3: Ch 3, dc in next 19 dc, (dc, ch 1, dc) in next ch, dc in next 40 dc, (dc, ch 1, dc) in next ch, dc in last 20 dc; join with slip st to first dc: 84 dc and 2 chs.

Rnd 4 (Increase rnd)**:** Ch 3, dc in next dc and in each dc across to next ch, (dc, ch 1, dc) in ch, dc in each st across to next ch, (dc, ch 1, dc) in ch, dc in each dc around; join with slip st to first dc: 88 dc and 2 chs.

Rnds 5-13: Repeat Rnd 4, 9 times: 124 dc and 2 chs.

Right Leg

Rnd 1: Ch 3, dc in next 30 dc, dc in ch of **both** front and back (skipping next 62 dc), dc in each dc around; join with slip st to first dc: 63 dc.

Rnds 2-5: Ch 3, dc in next dc and in each dc around; join with slip st to first dc.

Rnd 6: Ch 1, sc in same st as joining and in each dc around; join with slip st to first sc, finish off.

Left Leg

Rnd 1: With **right** side facing, join thread with slip st in ch of **both** front and back; ch 3, dc in next dc and in each dc around; join with slip st to first dc: 63 dc.

Rnds 2-6: Work same as Right Leg.

Using photo as a guide for placement, page 7, sew buttons to Trunks.

GENTLEMAN'S TRUNKS

Make same as Grandpa's Trunks, page 8, working in the following Stripe Sequence:
One rnd Blue, 2 rnds White; repeat these 3 rnds throughout.

Note: Carry color not being used loosely up side.

LADY'S BLOOMERS

Make Body same as Grandpa's Trunks, page 8, working Rnd 1 with Blue and remainder with White.

Right Leg

Rnd 1: Work same as Grandpa's Trunks: 63 dc.

Rnd 2 (Decrease rnd)**:** Ch 3, **[**(YO, insert hook in **next** dc, YO and pull up a loop, YO and draw through 2 loops on hook) twice, YO and draw through all 3 loops on hook **(decrease made, counts as one dc)]**, dc in next dc and in each dc around; join with slip st to first dc: 62 dc.

Rnds 3-5: Repeat Rnd 2, 3 times; at end of Rnd 5, finish off: 59 dc.

Rnd 6: With **right** side facing, join Blue with slip st in first st; ch 1, 2 sc in same st as joining, sc in each dc around; join with slip st to first sc, finish off: 60 sc.

EDGING

Rnd 1: With **right** side facing, join White with slip st in first st; ch 6, skip next 3 sc, ★ slip st in next sc, ch 6, skip next 3 sc; repeat from ★ around; join with slip st to joining slip st: 15 ch-6 sps.

Rnd 2: Ch 1, (sc, hdc, 2 dc, hdc, sc) in next ch-6 sp, slip st in next slip st, ★ (sc, hdc, 2 dc, hdc, sc) in next ch-6 sp, slip st in next slip st; repeat from ★ around.

Rnd 3: Ch 6, ★ working **behind** next ch-6, slip st around post of next slip st, ch 6; repeat from ★ around; join with slip st to first st.

Rnds 4-6: Repeat Rnds 2 and 3 once, then repeat Rnd 2 once **more**.

Finish off.

Left Leg

Rnd 1: Work same as Grandpa's Trunks: 63 dc.

Rnd 2: Ch 3, dc in next 30 dc, decrease, dc in next dc and in each dc around; join with slip st to first dc: 62 dc.

Rnds 3-5: Repeat Rnd 2, 3 times; at end of Rnd 5, finish off: 59 dc.

Complete same as Right Leg.

Waist Edging

With **right** side facing and working in free loops of beginning ch ***(Fig. 3, page 47)***, join White with slip st in any ch; ch 3, skip next ch, ★ slip st in next ch, ch 3, skip next ch; repeat from ★ around; join with slip st to joining slip st, finish off.

kitchen LACE

EASY

SHOPPING LIST

Thread (Lace Weight)

LACE 0

[284 yards (260 meters) per ball]:

- ☐ 1 ball

Crochet Hook

- ☐ Steel, size 7 (1.65 mm)
  or size needed for gauge

Additional Supplies

- ☐ 17" (43 cm) square piece of fabric
- ☐ ¼" (6 mm) wide Ribbon - 24" (61 cm)
- ☐ Sewing needle and thread

JAR LID COVER

Finished Size: To fit a
2½" (6.5 cm) diameter jar lid

Gauge Swatch:
2" (5 cm) diameter
Work same as Jar Lid Cover through Rnd 3: 26 ch-2 sps.

Ch 10; join with slip st to form a ring.

Rnd 1 (Right side)**:** Ch 3, 25 dc in ring; join with slip st to top of beginning ch-3: 26 sts.

Rnd 2: Ch 4, (dc in next dc, ch 1) around; join with slip st to third ch of beginning ch-4: 26 ch-1 sps.

Rnd 3: Slip st in next ch-1 sp, ch 5 (**counts as first dc plus ch 2, now and throughout**), dc in same sp, ch 2, skip next ch-1 sp, ★ (dc, ch 2) twice in next ch-1 sp, skip next ch-1 sp; repeat from ★ around; join with slip st to first dc.

Rnd 4: (Slip st, ch 5, dc) in next ch-2 sp, ch 2, sc in next ch-2 sp, ch 2, ★ (dc, ch 2) twice in next ch-2 sp, sc in next ch-2 sp, ch 2; repeat from ★ around; join with slip st to first dc: 39 sts and 39 ch-2 sps.

Rnd 5: (Slip st, ch 5, dc) in next ch-2 sp, ch 2, skip next ch-2 sp, sc in next sc, ch 2, skip next ch-2 sp, ★ (dc, ch 2) twice in next ch-2 sp, skip next ch-2 sp, sc in next sc, ch 2, skip next ch-2 sp; repeat from ★ around; join with slip st to first dc.

Rnd 6: (Slip st, ch 5, dc) in next ch-2 sp, ch 3, skip next ch-2 sp, sc in next sc, ch 3, skip next ch-2 sp, ★ (dc, ch 2, dc) in next ch-2 sp, ch 3, skip next ch-2 sp, sc in next sc, ch 3, skip next ch-2 sp; repeat from ★ around; join with slip st to first dc.

Rnd 7: (Slip st, ch 5, dc) in next ch-2 sp, ch 4, skip next ch-3 sp, sc in next sc, ch 4, skip next ch-3 sp, ★ (dc, ch 2, dc) in next ch-2 sp, ch 4, skip next ch-3 sp, sc in next sc, ch 4, skip next ch-3 sp; repeat from ★ around; join with slip st to first dc.

Rnds 8 and 9: (Slip st, ch 5, dc) in next ch-2 sp, ch 5, skip next sp, sc in next sc, ch 5, skip next sp, ★ (dc, ch 2, dc) in next ch-2 sp, ch 5, skip next sp, sc in next sc, ch 5, skip next sp; repeat from ★ around; join with slip st to first dc.

Rnds 10 and 11: (Slip st, ch 5, dc) in next ch-2 sp, ch 6, skip next sp, sc in next sc, ch 6, skip next sp, ★ (dc, ch 2, dc) in next ch-2 sp, ch 6, skip next sp, sc in next sc, ch 6, skip next sp; repeat from ★ around; join with slip st to first dc.

Rnd 12: (Slip st, ch 5, dc) in next ch-2 sp, ch 7, skip next ch-6 sp, sc in next sc, ch 7, skip next ch-6 sp, ★ (dc, ch 2, dc) in next ch-2 sp, ch 7, skip next ch-6 sp, sc in next sc, ch 7, skip next ch-6 sp; repeat from ★ around; join with slip st to first dc.

Rnd 13: Slip st in next ch-2 sp, ch 8, slip st in fourth ch from hook, ch 1, dc in same ch-2 sp, ch 7, slip next ch-7 sp, sc in next sc, ch 7, skip next ch-7 sp, ★ dc in next ch-2 sp, ch 5, slip st in fourth ch from hook, ch 1, dc in same ch-2 sp, ch 7, slip next ch-7 sp, sc in next sc, ch 7, skip next ch-7 sp; repeat from ★ around; join with slip st to third ch of beginning ch-8, finish off.

Weave ribbon through Rnd 9, gather to fit lid and tie ends in a bow.

BREAD CLOTH

Finished Size: 20" (51 cm) square

Gauge Swatch: 2" (5 cm) wide
Ch 21.
Row 1: Sc in second ch from hook and in each ch across.
Rows 2-10: Ch 1, turn; sc in each sc across.
Finish off.

Fold fabric over ¼" (6 mm) to the **wrong** side twice at each edge and sew in place. Press if desired.

Rnd 1 (Right side)**:** Working **over** hemmed edges, join thread with slip st in any corner of fabric; ch 1, work 163 sc evenly spaced across each edge of fabric; join with slip st to first sc: 652 sc.

Rnd 2: Ch 5, skip next 2 sc, dc in next sc, (ch 2, skip next 2 sc, dc in next dc) 53 times, ★ ch 2, dc in next sc, (ch 2, skip next 2 sc, dc in next sc) 54 times; repeat from ★ 2 times **more**, ch 1, sc in third ch of beginning ch-5 to form last ch-2 sp: 220 ch-2 sps.

Rnd 3: Ch 3, (dc, ch 2, 2 dc) in last ch-2 sp made, ch 4, skip next ch-2 sp, (2 dc, ch 2, 2 dc) in next ch-2 sp, **[**ch 4, skip next 2 ch-2 sps, (2 dc, ch 2, 2 dc) in next ch-2 sp**]** 17 times, ★ **[**ch 4, skip next ch-2 sp, (2 dc, ch 2, 2 dc) in next ch-2 sp**]** twice, **[**ch 4, skip next 2 ch-2 sps, (2 dc, ch 2, 2 dc) in next ch-2 sp**]** 17 times; repeat from ★ 2 times **more**, ch 2, skip last ch-2 sp, hdc in top of beginning ch-3 to form last ch-4 sp: 76 ch-2 sps and 76 ch-4 sps.

Rnd 4: Ch 1, sc in last ch-4 sp made, ch 2, (2 dc, ch 2) twice in next ch-2 sp, ★ sc in next ch-4 sp, ch 2, (2 dc, ch 2) twice in next ch-2 sp; repeat from ★ around; join with slip st to first sc: 228 ch-2 sps.

Rnd 5: Ch 1, sc in same st as joining, ch 2, skip next ch-2 sp, (2 dc, ch 2) twice in next ch-2 sp, skip next ch-2 sp, ★ sc in next sc, ch 2, skip next ch-2 sp, (2 dc, ch 2) twice in next ch-2 sp, skip next ch-2 sp; repeat from ★ around; join with slip st to first sc.

Rnd 6: Ch 1, sc in same st as joining, ch 3, skip next ch-2 sp, 2 dc in next ch-2 sp, ch 5, sc in fourth ch from hook, ch 1, 2 dc in same ch-2 sp, ch 3, skip next ch-2 sp, ★ sc in next sc, ch 3, skip next ch-2 sp, 2 dc in next ch-2 sp, ch 5, sc in fourth ch from hook, ch 1, 2 dc in same ch-2 sp, ch 3, skip next ch-2 sp; repeat from ★ around; join with slip st to first sc, finish off.

Designs by Eunice Svinicki.

beautiful BATH SET

EASY

SHOPPING LIST

Thread (Lace Weight)

LACE 0

[350 yards (320 meters) per ball]:

- ☐ 2 balls

Crochet Hook

- ☐ Steel, size 6 (1.8 mm) **or** size needed for gauge

Additional Supplies

- ☐ ¼" (6 mm) wide ribbon - 36" (91.5 cm)
- ☐ Tapestry needle
- ☐ 2" (5 cm) Plastic ring (for Tissue cover ONLY)

GAUGE INFORMATION

18 dc and 8 rows/rnds = 2" (5 cm)

Gauge Swatch: 2" (5 cm) square

Ch 20.

Row 1: Dc in fourth ch from hook and in each ch across **(3 skipped chs count as first dc)**: 18 dc.

Rows 2-8: Ch 3 **(counts as first dc)**, turn; dc in next dc and in each dc across.

Finish off.

STITCH GUIDE

TREBLE CROCHET
(abbreviated tr)

YO twice, insert hook in next dc, YO and pull up a loop (4 loops on hook), (YO and draw through 2 loops on hook) 3 times.

DOUBLE CROCHET 2 TOGETHER
(abbreviated dc2tog)
(uses next 2 dc)

★ YO, insert hook in **next** dc, YO and pull up a loop, YO and draw through 2 loops on hook; repeat from ★ once **more**, YO and draw through all 3 loops on hook **(counts as one dc)**.

SACHET BAG

Ch 81; being careful **not** to twist chain, join with slip st to form a ring.

Rnd 1 (Right side)**:** Ch 3 **(counts as first dc, now and throughout)**, dc in next ch and in each ch around; join with slip st to first dc: 81 dc.

Note: Loop a short piece of thread around any stitch to mark Rnd 1 as **right** side.

Rnd 2: Ch 3, turn; dc in next dc and in each dc around; join with slip st to first dc.

Rnd 3: Ch 3, turn; dc2tog, (dc in next dc, dc2tog) around; join with slip st to first dc: 54 dc.

Rnd 4: Ch 4 (**counts as first tr**), turn; tr in next dc and in each dc around; join with slip st to first tr.

Rnd 5: Ch 1, turn; sc in each tr around; join with slip st to first sc.

Rnd 6: Ch 3, turn; dc in next sc and in each sc around; join with slip st to first dc.

Rnds 7-15: Ch 3, turn; dc in next dc and in each dc around; join with slip st to first dc.

With **right** side together, flatten Bag matching dc; working through **both** thicknesses, ch 1, sc in each dc across; finish off.

Weave a 12" (30.5 cm) length of ribbon through Rnd 4 and tie in a bow.

MITT

Ch 88.

Row 1 (Right side)**:** Dc in fourth ch from hook **(3 skipped chs count as first dc)** and in next 16 chs (Cuff), ch 4, skip next 4 chs, dc in next 61 chs, sc in next 2 chs, 2 sc in last ch; working in free loops of beginning ch *(Fig. 3, page 47)*, sc in next 2 chs, dc in next 61 chs (Hand), ch 4, skip next 4 chs, dc in next 18 chs (Cuff); do **not** join: 164 sts and 2 ch-4 sps.

Note: Loop a short piece of thread around any stitch to mark Row 1 as **right** side.

Rows 2-14: Ch 3 (**counts as first dc, now and throughout**), turn; dc in next 17 dc, ch 4, skip next ch-4 sp, dc in next 61 dc, sc in next 6 sc, dc in next 61 dc, ch 4, skip next ch-4 sp, dc in last 18 dc.

Row 15: Ch 3, turn; dc in next 17 dc, ch 4, skip next ch-4 sp, dc in next 24 dc, ch 36 (Thumb), skip next 80 sts, dc in next 24 dc, ch 4, skip next ch-4 sp, dc in last 18 dc: 84 dc, 2 ch-4 sps, and 36 chs.

Row 16: Ch 3, turn; dc in next 17 dc, ch 4, skip next ch-4 sp, dc in next 24 dc and in next 16 chs, sc in next 4 chs, dc in next 16 chs and in next 24 dc, ch 4, skip next ch-4 sp, dc in last 18 dc: 120 sts and 2 ch-4 sps.

Rows 17-20: Ch 3, turn; dc in next 17 dc, ch 4, skip next ch-4 sp, dc in next 40 dc, sc in next 4 sc, dc in next 40 dc, ch 4, skip next ch-4 sp, dc in last 18 dc.

Finish off.

With **right** side together, sew seam around Thumb and Hand. Weave a 24" (61 cm) length of ribbon through ch-4 sps and tie in a bow.

TISSUE COVER

Rnd 1: Join thread with slip st around plastic ring; ch 1, work 78 sc around ring; join with slip st to first sc: 78 sc.

Rnd 2: Ch 1, turn; sc in each sc around; join with slip st to first sc.

Rnd 3 (Right side)**:** Ch 1, turn; sc in first 2 sc, skip next sc, (sc in next 2 sc, skip next sc) around; join with slip st to first sc: 52 sc.

Note: Loop a short piece of thread around any stitch to mark Rnd 3 as **right** side.

Rnd 4: Ch 1, turn; sc in first 6 sc, (2 dc, ch 2, 2 dc) in next sc, ★ sc in next 12 sc, (2 dc, ch 2, 2 dc) in next sc; repeat from ★ 2 times **more**, sc in last 6 sc; join with slip st to first sc: 48 sc, 16 dc, and 4 ch-2 sps.

Rnd 5: Ch 1, turn; sc in first 2 sc, dc in next 6 sts, (2 dc, ch 2, 2 dc) in next ch-2 sp, dc in next 6 sts, ★ sc in next 4 sc, dc in next 6 sts, (2 dc, ch 2, 2 dc) in next ch-2 sp, dc in next 6 sts; repeat from ★ 2 times **more**, sc in last 2 sc; join with slip st to first sc: 80 sts and 4 ch-2 sps.

Rnds 6-9: Ch 3 (**counts as first dc, now and throughout**), turn; ★ dc in next st and in each st across to next ch-2 sp, (2 dc, ch 2, 2 dc) in ch-2 sp; repeat from ★ 2 times **more**, dc in next st and in each st across; join with slip st to first dc: 144 dc and 4 ch-2 sps.

Rnd 10: Ch 3, turn; ★ dc in next dc and in each dc across to next ch-2 sp, 5 dc in ch-2 sp; repeat from ★ 3 times **more**, dc in next dc and in each dc across; join with slip st to first dc: 164 dc.

Rnds 11-17: Ch 3, turn; dc in next dc and in each dc around; join with slip st to first dc.

Rnd 18: Ch 4 **(counts as first tr)**, turn; tr in next dc and in each dc around; join with slip st to first tr.

Rnd 19: Ch 3, turn; dc in next tr and in each tr around; join with slip st to first dc.

Rnds 20-31: Ch 3, turn; dc in next dc and in each dc around; join with slip st to first dc.

Finish off.

Add Flowers if desired *(see Flowers)*.

Designs by Rheta Roach Lynch.

FLOWERS

A small amount of thread is required for **each** Flower.

Daisy

Rnd 1 (Right side)**:** With Yellow, ch 2, 8 hdc in second ch from hook; join with slip st to first hdc, finish off.

Note: Mark Rnd 1 as **right** side.

Rnd 2: With **right** side facing, join desired color with slip st in any hdc; ★ † ch 7, working in back ridge of chs ***(Fig. 1, page 47)***, sc in second ch from hook, hdc in next ch, dc in last 4 chs †, slip st in next hdc (**petal made**); repeat from ★ 6 times **more**, then repeat from † to † once; join with slip st to first slip st, finish off.

Daffodil

With Lt Yellow, ch 5; join with slip st to form a ring.

Rnd 1 (Right side)**:** ★ Ch 6, working in back ridge of chs *(Fig. 1, page 47)*, sc in second ch from hook, dc in last 4 chs, slip st in ring (**petal made**); repeat from ★ 5 times **more**; join with slip st to base of beginning ch-6, finish off.

Note: Mark Rnd 1 as **right** side.

Rnd 2: With **right** side facing, holding first petal made towards you and working in **front** of petals, skip first slip st, join Yellow with slip st in ring **before** next slip st; ch 3 (**counts as first dc**), (skip next slip st, dc in ring **before** next slip st) around; join with slip st to first dc, finish off.

Sunflower

With Brown, ch 4; join with slip st to form a ring.

Rnd 1 (Right side)**:** Ch 3 (**counts as first dc**), 11 dc in ring; join with slip st to first dc, finish off: 12 dc.

Note: Mark Rnd 1 as **right** side.

Rnd 2: With **right** side facing, join Yellow with slip st in any dc; ★ † ch 6, working in back ridge of chs *(Fig. 1, page 47)*, sc in second ch from hook, dc in last 4 chs (**petal made**) †, slip st in next dc on Rnd 1; repeat from ★ 10 times **more**, then repeat from † to † once; join with slip st to first slip st, finish off.

Designs by Terry Kimbrough.

fancy HANGER

EASY

SHOPPING LIST

Thread (Lace Weight)

[350 yards (320 meters) per ball]:

- ☐ 1 ball

Crochet Hook

- ☐ Steel, size 9 (1.4 mm) **or** size needed for gauge

Additional Supplies

- ☐ Satin covered hanger
- ☐ 1/8" (3 mm) wide ribbon - 27" (68.5 cm) length

GAUGE INFORMATION

Gauge Swatch: 1" (2.5 cm) diameter
Work same as Cover, page 26, through Rnd 2: 15 ch-1 sps.

COVER (Make 2)

Ch 4; join with slip st to form a ring.

Rnd 1 (Right side)**:** Ch 3 **(counts as first dc, now and throughout)**, 9 dc in ring; join with slip st to first dc: 10 dc.

Note: Loop a short piece of thread around any stitch to mark Rnd 1 as **right** side.

Rnd 2: Ch 4, dc in same st as joining, ch 1, dc in next dc, ch 1, ★ (dc, ch 1) twice in next dc, dc in next dc, ch 1; repeat from ★ around; join with slip st to third ch of beginning ch-4: 15 ch-1 sps.

Rnd 3: (Slip st, ch 3, 2 dc, ch 2, 3 dc) in next ch-1 sp, ch 1, skip next 2 ch-1 sps, ★ (3 dc, ch 2, 3 dc) in next ch-1 sp, ch 1, skip next 2 ch-1 sps; repeat from ★ around; join with slip st to first dc: 10 sps.

Rnd 4: Slip st in next 2 dc and in next ch-2 sp, ch 3, (2 dc, ch 2, 3 dc) in same sp, ch 4, skip next ch-1 sp, ★ (3 dc, ch 2, 3 dc) in next ch-2 sp, ch 4, skip next ch-1 sp; repeat from ★ around; join with slip st to first dc.

Rnd 5: Slip st in next 2 dc and in next ch-2 sp, ch 3, (2 dc, ch 2, 3 dc) in same sp, ch 3, working **around** next ch-4 ***(Fig. A)***, sc in ch-1 sp on Rnd 3, ch 3, ★ (3 dc, ch 2, 3 dc) in next ch-2 sp, ch 3, working **around** next ch-4, sc in ch-1 sp on Rnd 3, ch 3; repeat from ★ around; join with slip st to first dc: 15 sps.

Fig. A

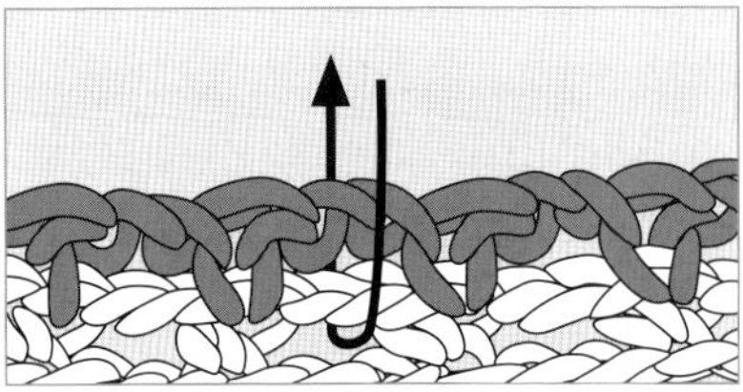

Rnd 6: Slip st in next 2 dc and in next ch-2 sp, ch 3, (2 dc, ch 2, 3 dc) in same sp, ch 3, skip next 2 ch-3 sps, ★ (3 dc, ch 2, 3 dc) in next ch-2 sp, ch 3, skip next 2 ch-3 sps; repeat from ★ around; join with slip st to first dc: 10 sps.

Rnd 7: Slip st in next 2 dc and in next ch-2 sp, ch 3, (2 dc, ch 2, 3 dc) in same sp, ch 4, skip next ch-3 sp, ★ (3 dc, ch 2, 3 dc) in next ch-2 sp, ch 4, skip next ch-3 sp; repeat from ★ around; join with slip st to first dc.

Rnd 8: Slip st in next 2 dc and in next ch-2 sp, ch 3, (2 dc, ch 2, 3 dc) in same sp, ch 3, working **around** next ch-4, sc in ch-3 sp on rnd **below**, ch 3, ★ (3 dc, ch 2, 3 dc) in next ch-2 sp, ch 3, working **around** next ch-4, sc in ch-3 sp on rnd **below**, ch 3; repeat from ★ around; join with slip st to first dc: 15 sps.

Rnds 9-32: Repeat Rnds 6-8, 8 times.

Rnd 33: Slip st in next 2 dc and in next ch-2 sp, ★ ch 8, skip next 2 ch-3 sps, slip st in next ch-2 sp; repeat from ★ around; join with slip st to third slip st, finish off.

Slip covers onto hanger and join together by weaving ribbon through ch-8 sps on Rnd 33; tie in a bow.

Add Flower(s) if desired ***(see Flowers, pages 22 and 23)***.

Design by Cathy Hardy.

pretty PURSE SET

EASY

SHOPPING LIST

Thread (Lace Weight)

LACE 0

[300 yards (274 meters) per ball]:

- ☐ 1 ball

Crochet Hook

- ☐ Steel, size 7 (1.65 mm) **or** size needed for gauge

Additional Supplies

- ☐ 1/8" (3 mm) wide ribbon - 12" (30.5 cm)
- ☐ 1" (2.5 cm) Split ring
- ☐ Satin - 7" x 10" (18 cm x 25.5 cm)
- ☐ Tapestry needle
- ☐ Sewing needle and thread
- ☐ Potpourri or fiberfill

GAUGE INFORMATION

In pattern, 2 repeats = 2½" (6.25 cm)

Gauge Swatch:
2⅝" wide x 2" high
(6.75 cm x 5 cm)

Ch 26.

Work same as Eyeglasses Case for 10 rows: 13 sts and 12 sps.

Finish off.

EYEGLASSES CASE

Ch 62.

Row 1: Sc in second ch from hook and in each ch across: 61 sc.

Row 2 (Right side)**:** Ch 1, turn; sc in first sc, ★ ch 3, skip next 5 sc, dc in next sc, (ch 1, dc in same st) 4 times, ch 3, skip next 5 sc, sc in next sc; repeat from ★ across: 31 sts and 30 sps.

Note: Loop a short piece of thread around any stitch to mark Row 2 as **right** side.

Row 3: Ch 3 **(counts as first dc, now and throughout)**, turn; 2 dc in first sc, ch 1, skip next ch-3 sp, sc in next ch-1 sp, (ch 3, sc in next ch-1 sp) 3 times, ch 1, skip next ch-3 sp, ★ (2 dc, ch 1) twice in next sc, skip next ch-3 sp, sc in next ch-1 sp, (ch 3, sc in next ch-1 sp) 3 times, ch 1, skip next ch-3 sp; repeat from ★ across to last sc, 3 dc in last sc.

Row 4: Ch 3, turn; 2 dc in first dc, ch 2, skip next ch-1 sp, sc in next ch-3 sp, (ch 3, sc in next ch-3 sp) twice, ch 2, skip next ch-1 sp, ★ (2 dc, ch 1, 2 dc) in next ch-1 sp, ch 2, skip next ch-1 sp, sc in next ch-3 sp, (ch 3, sc in next ch-3 sp) twice, ch 2, skip next ch-1 sp; repeat from ★ across to last 3 dc, skip next 2 dc, 3 dc in last dc.

Row 5: Ch 3, turn; 2 dc in first dc, ch 3, skip next ch-2 sp, (sc in next ch-3 sp, ch 3) twice, skip next ch-2 sp, ★ (2 dc, ch 1, 2 dc) in next ch-1 sp, ch 3, skip next ch-2 sp, (sc in next ch-3 sp, ch 3) twice, skip next ch-2 sp; repeat from ★ across to last 3 dc, skip next 2 dc, 3 dc in last dc.

Row 6: Ch 1, turn; sc in first dc, ch 3, skip next ch-3 sp, dc in next ch-3 sp, (ch 1, dc in same sp) 4 times, ch 3, skip next ch-3 sp, ★ sc in next ch-1 sp, ch 3, skip next ch-3 sp, dc in next ch-3 sp, (ch 1, dc in same sp) 4 times, ch 3, skip next ch-3 sp; repeat from ★ across to last 3 dc, skip next 2 dc, sc in last dc.

Rows 7-34: Repeat Rows 3-6, 7 times.

Do **not** finish off.

Lining

Using piece as a pattern and adding ½" (12 mm) along the top edge and ¼" (6 mm) seam allowances along remaining edges, cut satin. Fold top edge over ¼" (6 mm) to the wrong side twice and sew in place. With **right** sides together, sew a ¼" (6 mm) seam along side and bottom; turn right side out and press if desired.

Edging

Row 1: With **wrong** side together, working in end of rows and through **both** thicknesses, ch 1, 53 sc evenly spaced across to beginning ch; working in free loops of beginning ch ***(Fig. 3, page 47)*** **and** through both thicknesses, 3 sc in first ch, work 29 sc evenly spaced across; finish off: 85 sc.

Row 2: Join thread with sc in first sc of Row 1 ***(see Joining With Sc, page 47)***; ★ skip next 2 sc, dc in next sc, (ch 1, dc in same st) twice, skip next 2 sc, sc in next sc; repeat from ★ across; finish off.

Finishing

Insert Lining into piece and tack in place around top edge.

TISSUE COVER
First Side

Ch 50.

Row 1 (Right side)**:** Sc in second ch from hook and in each ch across: 49 sc.

Note: Loop a short piece of thread around any stitch to mark Row 1 as **right** side.

Row 2: Ch 1, turn; sc in each sc across.

Row 3: Ch 1, turn; sc in first sc, ★ ch 3, skip next 5 sc, dc in next sc, (ch 1, dc in same st) 4 times, ch 3, skip next 5 sc, sc in next sc; repeat from ★ across: 25 sts and 24 sps.

Row 4: Ch 3 (**counts as first dc, now and throughout**), turn; 2 dc in first sc, ch 1, skip next ch-3 sp, sc in next ch-1 sp, (ch 3, sc in next ch-1 sp) 3 times, ch 1, skip next ch-3 sp, ★ (2 dc, ch 1) twice in next sc, skip next ch-3 sp, sc in next ch-1 sp, (ch 3, sc in next ch-1 sp) 3 times, ch 1, skip next ch-3 sp; repeat from ★ 2 times **more**, 3 dc in last sc.

Row 5: Ch 3, turn; 2 dc in first dc, ch 2, skip next ch-1 sp, sc in next ch-3 sp, (ch 3, sc in next ch-3 sp) twice, ch 2, ★ skip next ch-1 sp, (2 dc, ch 1, 2 dc) in next ch-1 sp, ch 2, skip next ch-1 sp, sc in next ch-3 sp, (ch 3, sc in next ch-3 sp) twice, ch 2; repeat from ★ 2 times **more**, skip next ch-1 sp and next 2 dc, 3 dc in last dc.

Row 6: Ch 3, turn; 2 dc in first dc, ch 3, skip next ch-2 sp, (sc in next ch-3 sp, ch 3) twice, ★ skip next ch-2 sp, (2 dc, ch 1, 2 dc) in next ch-1 sp, ch 3, skip next ch-2 sp, (sc in next ch-3 sp, ch 3) twice; repeat from ★ 2 times **more**, skip next ch-2 sp and next 2 dc, 3 dc in last dc.

Row 7: Ch 1, turn; sc in first dc, ch 3, skip next ch-3 sp, dc in next ch-3 sp, (ch 1, dc in same sp) 4 times, ch 3, ★ skip next ch-3 sp, sc in next ch-1 sp, ch 3, skip next ch-3 sp, dc in next ch-3 sp, (ch 1, dc in same sp) 4 times, ch 3; repeat from ★ 2 times **more**, skip next ch-3 sp and next 2 dc, sc in last dc.

Rows 8-19: Repeat Rows 4-7, 3 times.

Finish off.

Second Side

Row 1: With **wrong** side facing and working in free loops of beginning ch *(Fig. 3, page 47)*, join thread with sc in first ch *(see Joining With Sc, page 47)*; sc in each ch across: 49 sc.

Rows 2-18: Work same as Rows 3-19 of First Side.

Do **not** finish off.

With **right** side facing and working in end of rows, sc evenly across; finish off.

With **right** side facing, join thread with slip st in last st of Row 19; ch 1, working in end of rows, sc evenly across; finish off.

Finishing

With **wrong** side together, last row of each side centered over beginning ch **and** working in inside loops, whipstitch ends together *(Fig. A)*.

Fig. A

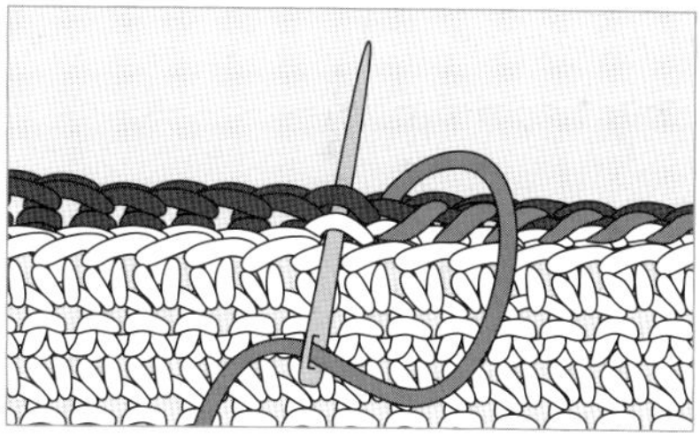

Turn **wrong** side out; with **right** sides together, fold corner with seam in center, sew across each corner ¼" (6 mm) from end *(Fig. B)*. Turn right side out.

Fig. B

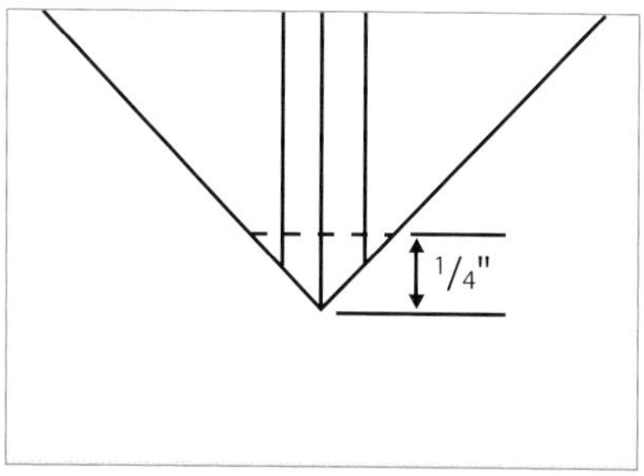

KEY FOB

First Side

Row 1 (Right side)**:** Ch 5 **(counts as first dc plus ch 1)**, dc in fifth ch from hook, (ch 1, dc in same ch) 3 times: 4 ch-1 sps.

Note: Loop a short piece of thread around any stitch to mark Row 1 as **right** side.

Row 2: Ch 1, turn; sc in first ch-1 sp, (ch 3, sc in next ch-1 sp) 3 times: 3 ch-3 sps.

Row 3: Ch 1, turn; sc in first ch-3 sp, (ch 3, sc in next ch-3 sp) twice: 2 ch-3 sps.

Row 4: Ch 1, turn; sc in first ch-3 sp, ch 3, sc in last ch-3 sp, slip st in third ch of same ch-3 sp and in last sc: one ch-3 sp.

Row 5: Ch 4 **(counts as first dc plus ch 1)**, turn; dc in first ch-3 sp on Row 3, (ch 1, dc in same sp) 3 times, ch 1, sc in ch-3 sp on Row 4, ch 1, skip next sc, dc in next ch-3 sp on Row 3, (ch 1, dc in same sp) 4 times: 10 ch-1 sps.

Row 6: Ch 1, turn; sc in first ch-1 sp, (ch 3, sc in next ch-1 sp) 3 times, skip next ch-1 sp, sc in next sc, skip next ch-1 sp, sc in next ch-1 sp, (ch 3, sc in next ch-1 sp) 3 times: 6 ch-3 sps.

Row 7: Ch 1, turn; sc in first ch-3 sp, (ch 3, sc in next ch-3 sp) twice, slip st in same sp, skip next sc, sc in next sc, (slip st, sc) in next ch-3 sp, (ch 3, sc in next ch-3 sp) twice: 4 ch-3 sps.

Row 8: Ch 1, turn; sc in first ch-3 sp, ch 3, sc in next ch-3 sp, slip st in same sp, skip next sc and next slip st, slip st in next sc, skip next slip st and next sc, slip st in next ch-3 sp, sc in same sp, ch 3, sc in last ch-3 sp; do **not** finish off.

EDGING

Rnd 1: Ch 1, turn; 5 sc in first ch-3 sp, slip st in next sc, slip st in next 3 slip sts and in next sc, 5 sc in last ch-3 sp, sc in last sc; working in sps at end of rows, 2 sc in each of next 2 sps, 4 sc in next dc row, 2 sc in next sp, 4 sc in next dc row, 3 sc in beginning ch (tip), 4 sc in next dc row, 2 sc in next sp, 4 sc in next dc row, 2 sc in each of next 2 sps, sc in next sc; join with slip st to first sc: 43 sc.

Rnd 2: Ch 1, do **not** turn; sc in first 5 sc, slip st in next 5 slip sts, sc in next 20 sc, 2 sc in next sc, 3 sc in next sc (tip), 2 sc in next sc, sc in each sc around; join with slip st to first sc, finish off: 47 sc.

Lining

Using First Side as a pattern and adding ¼" (6 mm) seam allowance, cut 2 pieces of satin. With **right** sides together, sew a ¼" (6 mm) seam leaving an opening for turning. Clip curves and corners; turn right side out. Fill with potpourri or fiberfill stuffing; sew opening closed.

Second Side

Work same as First Side through Edging Rnd 2; do **not** finish off.

Rnd 3: Ch 1; with **wrong** sides together, matching sts and working through **both** pieces, sc in first 5 sc, slip st in next 5 slip sts, sc in next sc, place marker around last sc made for Ruffle placement, sc in each sc around inserting lining before closing; join with slip st to first sc, finish off.

Ruffle: With **right** side facing, join thread with slip st in marked sc; ★ dc in next sc, (ch 1, dc in same st) twice, slip st in next sc; repeat from ★ around to last 5 slip sts, leave remaining slip sts unworked; finish off.

Finishing

Join ribbon to split ring with a slip knot. Thread tapestry needle with ribbon and weave through center slip st at top of Heart. Tie in a bow.

Designs by Anita Lewis.

towel TRIMMINGS

EASY

Finished Size for each Trim:
20½" long x 1" high (52 cm x 2.5 cm)

SHOPPING LIST

Thread (Lace Weight)

LACE 0

[350 yards (320 meters) per ball]:

- ☐ 1 ball

Crochet Hook

- ☐ Steel, size 6 (1.8 mm) **or** size needed for gauge

Additional Supplies

- ☐ Kitchen or hand towels
- ☐ Sewing needle and thread

GAUGE INFORMATION

Gauge Swatch: 2" (5 cm) wide
Ch 19.
Row 1: Sc in second ch from hook and in each ch across: 18 sc.
Rows 2-8: Ch 1, turn; sc in each sc across.
Finish off.

TRIM #1

(Multiple of 4 chs)

Ch 184.

Row 1 (Right side)**:** Dc in sixth ch from hook, ★ ch 1, skip next ch, dc in next ch; repeat from ★ across: 90 sps.

Note: Loop a short piece of thread around any stitch to mark Row 1 as **right** side.

Row 2: Ch 3, turn; dc in next ch-1 sp, dc in each dc and in each ch-1 sp across, dc in next ch: 181 sts.

1
2
3

Row 3: Turn; slip st in first 3 dc, ch 3, 3 dc in same st, ch 3, **turn**; dc in top of beginning ch-3 to form loop, ch 3, **turn**; 4 dc in same loop, skip next 3 dc on Row 2, 4 dc in next dc, ★ ch 3, **turn**; dc in top of first dc of 4-dc group just made to form loop, ch 3, **turn**; 4 dc in same loop, skip next 3 dc on Row 2, 4 dc in next dc; repeat from ★ across to last 2 sts, leave last 2 sts unworked; finish off.

TRIM #2

(Multiple of 9 chs plus 6)

Ch 186.

Row 1 (Right side)**:** Dc in fourth ch from hook and in each ch across: 184 sts.

Note: Loop a short piece of thread around any stitch to mark Row 1 as **right** side.

Row 2: Ch 1, turn; sc in each st across.

Row 3: Ch 5 **(counts as first dc plus ch 2)**, turn; skip next 2 sc, dc in next sc, ★ ch 2, skip next 2 sc, dc in next sc; repeat from ★ across: 61 ch-2 sps.

Row 4: Ch 3 **(counts as first dc)**, turn; 2 dc in next ch-2 sp, dc in next dc, ★ (ch 2, dc in next dc) twice, 2 dc in next ch-2 sp, dc in next dc; repeat from ★ across.

Row 5: Ch 1, turn; sc in first 4 dc, ★ (sc, ch 3, slip st in sc just made) twice in next ch-2 sp, sc in next ch-2 sp, ch 3, slip st in sc just made, sc in same sp and in next 4 dc; repeat from ★ across; finish off.

TRIM #3

(Multiple of 4 chs plus 3)

Ch 183.

Row 1 (Right side)**:** Dc in fourth ch from hook and in each ch across: 181 sts.

Note: Loop a short piece of thread around any stitch to mark Row 1 as **right** side.

Row 2: Ch 4 (**counts as first dc plus ch 1**), turn; ★ skip next dc, dc in next dc, ch 1; repeat from ★ across to last 2 sts, skip next dc, dc in last st: 90 ch-1 sps.

Row 3: Ch 3, turn; dc in each ch-1 sp and in each dc across: 181 sts.

Row 4: Ch 1, turn; sc in first dc, ★ ch 5, skip next 3 dc, sc in next st; repeat from ★ across: 45 ch-5 sps.

Row 5: Ch 1, turn; (sc, ch 2, 4 dc) in each ch-5 sp across.

Row 6: Turn; slip st in first 4 dc and in top of next ch-2, ch 1, sc in same st, ★ ch 5, skip next 5 sts, sc in top of next ch-2; repeat from ★ across: 44 ch-5 sps.

Row 7: Ch 5, turn; slip st in fourth ch from hook, 4 dc in next ch-5 sp, ★ sc in next ch-5 sp, ch 5, slip st in fourth ch from hook, 4 dc in same ch-5 sp; repeat from ★ across; finish off.

FINISHING

Washing & Blocking

For a more professional look, Trims should be washed and blocked. Using a mild detergent and warm water and being careful not to rub, twist, or wring, gently squeeze suds through each one. Rinse several times in cool, clear water. Roll in a clean terry towel and gently press out the excess moisture. Lay on a flat surface and shape to proper size; pin in place using rust-proof pins where needed. Allow to dry **completely**.

Using photo as a guide, page 37, place Trim along hemline on right side, folding ends to wrong side, and baste in place. Hand sew or machine sew to secure. Remove basting thread.

Designs by C. Strohmeyer.

spider FILET VALANCE

EASY

SHOPPING LIST

Thread (Lace Weight) LACE 0

[350 yards (320 meters) per ball]:

☐ 4 balls

Crochet Hook

☐ Steel, size 6 (1.8 mm) **or** size needed for gauge

Finished Size: 47" wide x 14" long (119.5 cm x 35.5 cm)

GAUGE INFORMATION

In pattern, (dc, ch 2) 6 times (18 sts)
and 8 rows = 2" (5 cm)

Gauge Swatch: 3" (7.5 cm) square

Ch 29.

Row 1: Dc in fourth ch from hook **(3 skipped chs count as first dc)** and in each ch across: 27 dc.

Rows 2-12: Ch 3 (**counts as first dc**), turn; dc in next dc and in each dc across.

Finish off.

To adjust the length of the Valance by 2½" (6.25 cm), add or subtract 24 chs to the beginning ch for a difference of 24 dc in Row 1.

STITCH GUIDE

TREBLE CROCHET

(abbreviated tr)

YO twice, insert hook in st or sp indicated, YO and pull up a loop (4 loops on hook), (YO and draw through 2 loops on hook) 3 times.

VALANCE

Ch 119.

Row 1 (Right side)**:** Dc in eighth ch from hook, ch 2, skip next 2 chs, dc in next ch and in each ch across: 110 dc.

Note: Loop a short piece of thread around any stitch to mark Row 1 as **right** side.

Row 2: Ch 5 **(counts as first dc plus ch 2, now and throughout)**, turn; skip next 2 dc, dc in next 4 dc, ★ ch 2, (skip next 2 dc, dc in next dc, ch 2) 6 times, skip next 2 dc, dc in next 4 dc; repeat from ★ 2 times **more**, (ch 2, skip next 2 dc, dc in next dc) 10 times, ch 2, dc in next dc, ch 2, skip next 2 chs, dc in next ch: 47 dc and 34 ch-2 sps.

Row 3: Ch 5, turn; dc in next dc, ch 2, dc in next dc, (2 dc in next ch-2 sp, dc in next dc) 5 times, (ch 2, dc in next dc) 4 times, 2 dc in next ch-2 sp, dc in next dc, ch 4, skip next 2 dc, dc in next dc, 2 dc in next ch-2 sp, ★ dc in next dc, (ch 2, dc in next dc) 5 times, 2 dc in next ch-2 sp, dc in next dc, ch 4, skip next 2 dc, dc in next dc, 2 dc in next ch-2 sp; repeat from ★ across to last dc, (dc, ch 2, tr) in last dc.

Row 4: Ch 6, turn; dc in first tr, ★ 2 dc in next ch-2 sp, dc in next dc, ch 5, tr in next ch-4 sp, ch 5, skip next 3 dc, dc in next dc, 2 dc in next ch-2 sp, dc in next dc, (ch 2, dc in next dc) 3 times; repeat from ★ 3 times **more**, ch 14, skip next 14 dc, dc in next dc, (ch 2, dc in next dc) twice.

Row 5: Ch 5, turn; dc in next dc, ch 2, dc in next dc and in next 14 chs, (dc in next dc, ch 2) twice, ★ † dc in next dc, 2 dc in next ch-2 sp, dc in next dc, ch 7, sc in next ch-5 sp, sc in next tr and in next ch-5 sp, ch 7, skip next 3 dc, dc in next dc †, 2 dc in next ch-2 sp, dc in next dc, ch 2; repeat from ★ 2 times **more**, then repeat from † to † once, 2 dc in last sp, (dc, ch 2, tr) in fourth ch of beginning ch-6.

Row 6: Ch 6, turn; dc in first tr, 2 dc in next ch-2 sp, dc in next dc, ★ ch 7, sc in next ch-7 sp, sc in next 3 sc and in next ch-7 sp, ch 7, skip next 3 dc, dc in next dc, 2 dc in next ch-2 sp, dc in next dc; repeat from ★ 3 times **more**, ch 2, dc in next dc, (ch 2, skip next 2 dc, dc in next dc) 5 times, (ch 2, dc in next dc) twice.

Row 7: Ch 5, turn; dc in next dc, ch 2, dc in next dc, (2 dc in next ch-2 sp, dc in next dc) 5 times, ch 2, dc in next dc, ch 2, skip next 2 dc, dc in next dc, ★ 3 dc in next ch-7 sp, ch 7, sc in next 5 sc, ch 7, 3 dc in next ch-7 sp, dc in next dc, ch 2, skip next 2 dc, dc in next dc; repeat from ★ across to beginning ch-6, leave beginning ch unworked.

Row 8: Turn; slip st in first 4 sts, ch 5, ★ skip next 2 dc, dc in next dc, 3 dc in next ch-7 sp, ch 5, skip next sc, sc in next 3 sc, ch 5, 3 dc in next ch-7 sp, dc in next dc, ch 2, skip next 2 dc, (dc in next dc, ch 2) twice; repeat from ★ 3 times **more**, dc in next dc, ch 14, skip next 14 dc, dc in next dc, (ch 2, dc in next dc) twice.

Row 9: Ch 5, turn; dc in next dc, ch 2, dc in next dc, dc in next 14 chs and in next dc, ★ (ch 2, dc in next dc) 3 times, ch 2, skip next 2 dc, dc in next dc, 3 dc in next ch-5 sp, ch 1, skip next sc, tr in next sc, ch 1, 3 dc in next ch-5 sp, dc in next dc, ch 2, skip next 2 dc, dc in next dc; repeat from ★ across to beginning ch-5, leave beginning ch unworked.

Row 10: Turn; slip st in first 4 sts, ch 5, skip next 2 dc, dc in next dc, dc in next 2 ch-1 sps, dc in next dc, ch 2, skip next 2 dc, dc in next dc, ★ ch 2, (dc in next dc, ch 2) 5 times, skip next 2 dc, dc in next dc, dc in next 2 ch-1 sps, dc in next dc, ch 2, skip next 2 dc, dc in next dc; repeat from ★ 2 times **more**, (ch 2, dc in next dc) 4 times, (ch 2, skip next 2 dc, dc in next dc) 5 times, (ch 2, dc in next dc) twice.

Repeat Rows 3-10 until piece measures approximately 46½" (118 cm) **or desired width**, ending by working Row 10.

Last Row: Ch 5, turn; dc in next dc, ch 2, dc in next dc and in each ch and each dc across.

Edging: Ch 1, working in end of rows, skip first row, (sc in next row, ch 1) twice, ★ (dc, ch 1) 7 times in next row, sc in next row, ch 1; repeat from ★ across to last 2 rows, sc in next row, ch 1, slip st in beginning ch; finish off.

Design by Eunice Svinicki.

general INSTRUCTIONS

ABBREVIATIONS

ch(s)	chain(s)
cm	centimeters
dc	double crochet(s)
dc2tog	double crochet 2 together
dc3tog	double crochet 3 together
hdc	half double crochet(s)
mm	millimeters
Rnd(s)	Round(s)
sc	single crochet(s)
sp(s)	space(s)
st(s)	stitch(es)
tr	treble crochet(s)
YO	yarn over

SYMBOLS & TERMS

★ — work instructions following ★ as many **more** times as indicated in addition to the first time.

† to † — work all instructions from first † to second † **as many** times as specified.

( ) or **[ ]** — work enclosed instructions **as many** times as specified by the number immediately following **or** work all enclosed instructions in the stitch or space indicated **or** contains explanatory remarks.

colon (:) — the number(s) given after a colon at the end of a row or round denote(s) the number of stitches or spaces you should have on that row or round.

CROCHET TERMINOLOGY		
UNITED STATES		INTERNATIONAL
slip stitch (slip st)	=	single crochet (sc)
single crochet (sc)	=	double crochet (dc)
half double crochet (hdc)	=	half treble crochet (htr)
double crochet (dc)	=	treble crochet (tr)
treble crochet (tr)	=	double treble crochet (dtr)
double treble crochet (dtr)	=	triple treble crochet (ttr)
triple treble crochet (tr tr)	=	quadruple treble crochet (qtr)
skip	=	miss

GAUGE

Exact gauge is **essential** for proper size. Before beginning your project, make the sample swatch given in the individual instructions in the thread and hook specified. After completing the swatch, measure it, counting your stitches and rows/rounds carefully. If your swatch is larger or smaller than specified, **make another, changing hook size to get the correct gauge**. Keep trying until you find the size hook that will give you the specified gauge.

STEEL CROCHET HOOKS																
U.S.	00	0	1	2	3	4	5	6	7	8	9	10	11	12	13	14
Metric - mm	3.5	3.25	2.75	2.25	2.1	2	1.9	1.8	1.65	1.5	1.4	1.3	1.1	1	.85	.75

BEGINNER	Projects for first-time crocheters using basic stitches. Minimal shaping.
EASY	Projects using yarn with basic stitches, repetitive stitch patterns, simple color changes, and simple shaping and finishing.
INTERMEDIATE	Projects using a variety of techniques, such as basic lace patterns or color patterns, mid-level shaping and finishing.
EXPERIENCED	Projects with intricate stitch patterns, techniques and dimension, such as non-repeating patterns, multi-color techniques, fine threads, small hooks, detailed shaping and refined finishing.

Yarn Weight Symbol & Names	LACE 0	SUPER FINE 1	FINE 2	LIGHT 3	MEDIUM 4	BULKY 5	SUPER BULKY 6	JUMBO 7
Type of Yarns in Category	Fingering, size 10 crochet thread	Sock, Fingering, Baby	Sport, Baby	DK, Light Worsted	Worsted, Afghan, Aran	Chunky, Craft, Rug	Super Bulky, Roving	Jumbo, Roving
Crochet Gauge* Ranges in Single Crochet to 4" (10 cm)	32-42 sts**	21-32 sts	16-20 sts	12-17 sts	11-14 sts	8-11 sts	6-9 sts	5 sts and fewer
Advised Hook Size Range	Steel*** 6 to 8, Regular hook B-1	B-1 to E-4	E-4 to 7	7 to I-9	I-9 to K-10½	K-10½ to M/N-13	M/N-13 to Q	Q and larger

*GUIDELINES ONLY: The chart above reflects the most commonly used gauges and hook sizes for specific yarn categories.

** Lace weight yarns are usually crocheted with larger hooks to create lacy openwork patterns. Accordingly, a gauge range is difficult to determine. Always follow the gauge stated in your pattern.

*** Steel crochet hooks are sized differently from regular hooks–the higher the number, the smaller the hook, which is the reverse of regular hook sizing.

JOINING WITH SC

When instructed to join with a sc, begin with a slip knot on the hook. Insert the hook in stitch or space indicated, YO and pull up a loop, YO and draw through both loops on hook.

BACK RIDGE OF A CHAIN

Work only in loops indicated by arrows *(Fig. 1)*.

Fig. 1

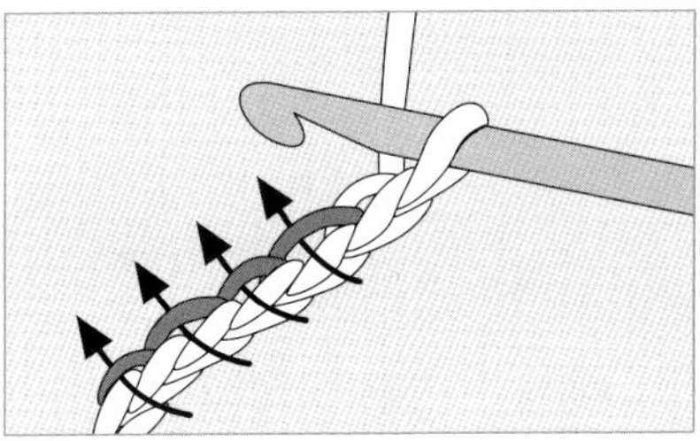

BACK LOOP ONLY

Work only in loop(s) indicated by arrow *(Fig. 2)*.

Fig. 2

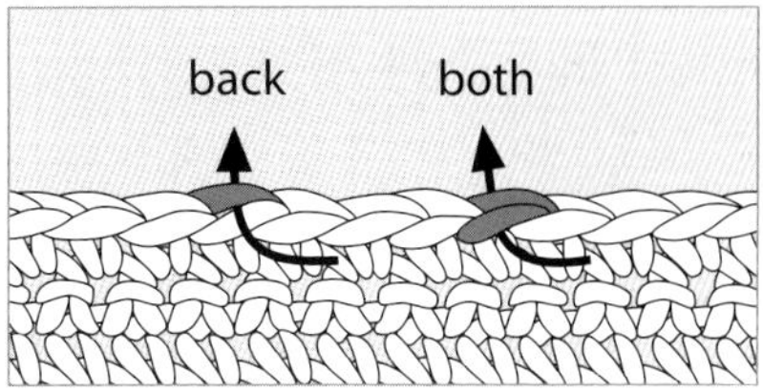

FREE LOOPS OF A CHAIN

When instructed to work in free loops of a chain, work in loop indicated by arrow *(Fig. 3)*.

Fig. 3

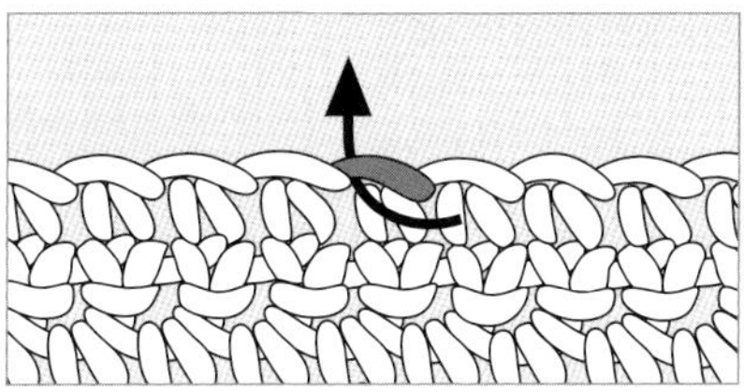

THREAD INFORMATION

Each project in this book was made using Lace Weight Cotton Thread (size 10). Any brand of Lace Weight Cotton Thread may be used.

For your convenience, listed below are the thread styles and colors used to create our photography models. Because thread manufacturers make frequent changes in their product lines, you may sometimes find it necessary to use a substitute thread or to search for the discontinued product at alternate suppliers (locally or online).

FLORAL SUNCATCHER
Aunt Lydia's® Crochet Thread™
#424 Peach

VINTAGE "DRAWERS"
Aunt Lydia's® Crochet Thread™
Blue - #486 Navy
White - #1 White

KITCHEN LACE
DMC Cebelia® size 10
Ecru

BEAUTIFUL BATH SET
Aunt Lydia's® Crochet Thread™
#435 Silver

FLOWERS
Aunt Lydia's® Crochet Thread™
#1 White, #421 Goldenrod, #422 Golden Yellow, #131 Fudge Brown, #856 Peacock and #493 French Rose

FANCY HANGER
Aunt Lydia's® Crochet Thread™
#856 Peacock

PRETTY PURSE SET
Aunt Lydia's® Crochet Thread™
#995 Ocean

TOWEL TRIMMINGS
Southmaid®
#494 Victory Red

SPIDER FILET VALANCE
Aunt Lydia's® Crochet Thread™
#480 Delft

We have made every effort to ensure that these instructions are accurate and complete. We cannot, however, be responsible for human error, typographical mistakes, or variations in individual work.

Production Team: Instructional/Technical Editor - Linda A. Daley; Editorial Writer - Susan Frantz Wiles; Senior Graphic Artist - Lora Puls; Photo Stylist - Lori Wenger; and Photographer - Jason Masters.